CHEYENNE
History and Culture

Helen Dwyer and D. L. Birchfield

Consultant Robert J. Conley
Sequoyah Distinguished Professor at Western Carolina University

Gareth Stevens
Publishing

Please visit our website, **www.garethstevens.com**. For a free color catalog of all our high-quality books, call toll free 1-800-542-2595 or fax 1-877-542-2596.

Library of Congress Cataloging-in-Publication Data

Dwyer, Helen.
Cheyenne history and culture / Helen Dwyer and D. L. Birchfield.
    p. cm. — (Native American library)
Includes index.
ISBN 978-1-4339-6666-8 (pbk.)
ISBN 978-1-4339-6667-5 (6-pack)
ISBN 978-1-4339-6664-4 (library binding)
1. Cheyenne Indians—History. 2. Cheyenne Indians—Social life and customs. I. Birchfield, D. L., 1948- II. Title.
E99.C53D89 2012
978.004'97353—dc23

                         2011026008

New edition published in 2012 by
Gareth Stevens Publishing
111 East 14th Street, Suite 349
New York, NY 10003

First edition published 2005 by Gareth Stevens Publishing

Copyright © 2012 Gareth Stevens Publishing

Produced by Discovery Books
Project editor: Helen Dwyer
Designer and page production: Sabine Beaupré
Photo researchers: Tom Humphrey and Helen Dwyer
Maps: Stefan Chabluk

Photo credits: Corbis: pp. 5, 8 (Bettmann), 20, 23 (bottom), 27 (top), 37 (Chris Farina); Native Stock: pp. 15 (bottom), 18 (both), 19, 21 (bottom), 22 (both), 23 (top), 24, 25 (both), 26, 31, 32, 33, 35 (both), 39; North Wind Picture Archives: p.12; Peter Newark's American Pictures: pp. 13, 14, 15 (top), 16, 17, 21 (top and middle), 27 (bottom); Shutterstock: pp. 5 (Kenneth Keifer), 28 (Lars Christensen), 29 (Steve Byland), 30 (hjschneider); Wikimedia: pp. 7 (J. Gurney & Son), 36 (Becky Meyer/Red Earth Festival), 38 (Bill Koplitz/FEMA Photo Library).

Printed in the United States of America

CPSIA compliance information: Batch #CW12GS: For further information contact Gareth Stevens, New York, New York at 1-800-542-2595.

CONTENTS

Words that appear in the glossary are printed in **boldface** type the first time they appear in the text.

INTRODUCTION

The Cheyennes are a people originally from the Great Lakes region. They are just one of the many groups of Native Americans who live today in North America. There are well over five hundred Native American tribes in the United States and more than six hundred in Canada. At least three million people in North America consider themselves to be Native Americans. But who are Native Americans, and how do the Cheyennes fit into the history of North America's native peoples?

Siberia (Asia) and Alaska (North America) are today separated by an area of ocean named the Bering Strait. During the last ice age, the green area on this map was at times dry land. The Asian ancestors of the Cheyennes walked from one continent to the other.

THE FIRST IMMIGRANTS

Native Americans are people whose **ancestors** settled in North America thousands of years ago. These ancestors probably came from eastern parts of Asia. Their **migrations** probably occurred during cold periods called **ice ages**. At these times, sea levels were much lower than they are now. The area between northeastern Asia and Alaska was dry land, so it was possible to walk between the continents.

Scientists are not sure when these migrations took place, but it must have been more than twelve thousand years ago. Around that time, water levels rose and covered the land between Asia and the Americas.

4

By around ten thousand years ago, the climate had warmed and was similar to conditions today. The first peoples in North America moved around the continent in small groups, hunting wild animals and collecting a wide variety of plant foods. Gradually these groups spread out and lost contact with each other. They developed separate **cultures** and adopted lifestyles that suited their **environments.**

The Cliff Palace at Mesa Verde, Colorado, is the most spectacular example of Native American culture that survives today. It consists of more than 150 rooms and pits built around A.D. 1200 from sandstone blocks.

SETTLING DOWN

Although many tribes continued to gather food and hunt or fish, some Native Americans began to live in settlements and grow crops. Their homes ranged from underground pit houses and huts of mud and thatch to dwellings in cliffs. By 3500 B.C., a plentiful supply of fish in the Pacific Ocean and in rivers had enabled people to settle in large coastal villages from Alaska to Washington State. In the deserts of Arizona more than two thousand years later, farmers constructed hundreds of miles of **irrigation** canals to carry water to their crops.

Before 1700, the Cheyennes were living in wooded regions near the Great Lakes, in what is present-day Minnesota. They survived by hunting, fishing, and farming. In the early 1700s, they were driven westward then southward by enemy tribes and became buffalo hunters on the Great Plains.

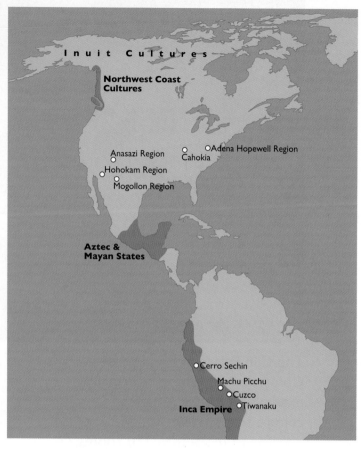

In the Ohio River valley between 700 B.C. and A.D. 500, people of the Adena and Hopewell cultures built clusters of large burial mounds, such as the Serpent Mound in Ohio, which survives today. In the Mississippi **floodplains**, the native peoples formed complex societies. They created mud and thatch temples on top of flat earth pyramids. Their largest town, Cahokia, in Illinois, contained more than one hundred mounds and may have been home to thirty thousand people.

This map highlights some of the main early Native American cultures.

CONTACT WITH EUROPEANS

Around A.D. 1500, European ships reached North America. The first explorers were the Spanish. Armed with guns and riding horses, they took over land and forced the Native Americans to work for them. The Spanish were followed by the British, Dutch, and French, who were all looking for land to settle and for opportunities to trade.

When Native Americans met these Europeans they came into contact with diseases, such as smallpox and measles, that they had never experienced before. At least one half of all Native Americans, and possibly many more than that, were unable to overcome these diseases and died.

Guns were also disastrous for Native Americans. At first, only the Europeans had guns, which enabled them to overcome native peoples in fights and battles. Eventually, Native American groups obtained guns and used them in conflicts with each other. Native American groups were also forced to take sides and fight in wars between the French and British.

Cheyenne chief Little Robe (1828–1886), photographed in 1871. He became a chief in 1863.

Horses, too, had a big influence in Native American lifestyles, especially on the Great Plains. Some groups became horse breeders and traders. People were able to travel greater distances and began to hunt buffalo on horseback. Soon horses became central to Plains trade and social life.

The Cheyennes acquired horses around 1760. The horses made their buffalo-hunting lifestyle much easier, and the tribe soon became very powerful.

At the end of the 1700s, people of European descent began to migrate over the Appalachian Mountains, looking for new land to farm and exploit. By the middle of the nineteenth century, they had reached the west coast of North America. This expansion was disastrous for Native Americans.

The Cheyennes were not affected by white settlers until the middle of the nineteenth century. Then in 1849, many Cheyennes caught a disease called **cholera** from Europeans. A few years later, the United States began a war with the Southern Cheyennes.

RESERVATION LIFE

Many native peoples were pressured into moving onto **reservations** to the west. The biggest of these reservations later became the U.S. state of Oklahoma. Native Americans who tried to remain in their homelands were attacked and defeated.

In 1869, the Southern Cheyennes were forced to move to a reservation in Oklahoma. Despite resisting for several years, the Northern Cheyennes were also forced onto the reservation, but some of them were allowed to move to a reservation in Montana in 1884.

New laws in the United States and Canada took away most of the control Native Americans had over their lives. They were expected to give up their cultures and adopt the ways and habits of white Americans. It became a crime to practice their traditional religions. Children were taken from their homes and placed in **boarding schools**, where they were forbidden to speak their native languages.

Despite this **persecution**, many Native Americans clung on to their cultures through the first half of the twentieth century.

The Society of American Indians was founded in 1911 and its campaign for U.S. citizenship for Native Americans was successful in 1924. Other Native American organizations were formed to promote traditional cultures and to campaign politically for Native American rights.

John Wooden Legs and President Lyndon Johnson in 1967. John Wooden Legs (1909–1981) was the tribal president of the Cheyennes from 1955 to 1968. In 1975, he founded Chief Dull Knife College in Lame Deer, Montana.

THE ROAD TO SELF-GOVERNMENT

Despite these campaigns, Native Americans on reservations endured **poverty** and very low standards of living. Many of them moved away to work and live in cities, where they hoped life would be better. In most cases, they found life there just as difficult. They not only faced **discrimination** and **prejudice** but also could not compete successfully for jobs against more established ethnic groups.

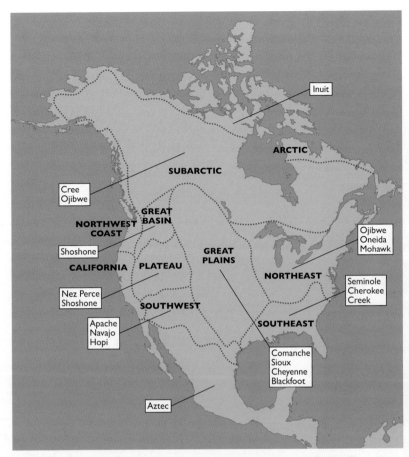

This map of North America highlights the main Native American cultural groups, along with the smaller groups, or tribes, featured in this series of books.

In the 1970s, the American Indian Movement (AIM) organized large protests that attracted attention worldwide. They highlighted the problems of unemployment, discrimination, and poverty that Native Americans experienced in North America.

The AIM protests led to changes in policy. Some new laws protected the civil rights of Native Americans, while other laws allowed tribal governments to be formed. Today tribal governments have a wide range of powers. They operate large businesses and run their own schools and health care.

LAND AND ORIGINS

Chapter 1

LAND OF THE CHEYENNES

The Cheyennes are a North American native people who became one of the most famous tribes of the Great Plains during the nineteenth century. Today, about eight thousand Northern Cheyennes live on the Northern Cheyenne Reservation in Montana. About five thousand Southern Cheyennes live in Oklahoma, mostly on or near the Concho Reservation, which they share with the Southern Arapaho tribe.

The Cheyennes' name for themselves is *Tsetschestahase,* meaning "people who are alike" or "our people." The name *Cheyenne* derives from a Sioux word, *Shai-ena,* meaning "people of an **alien** speech."

THE CHEYENNE ORIGIN STORY

No one knows exactly how the Cheyennes and other Native American peoples came to North America, but like many of these cultures, traditional Cheyennes explain their arrival in an origin story. According to this story, all things were formed by a Creator,

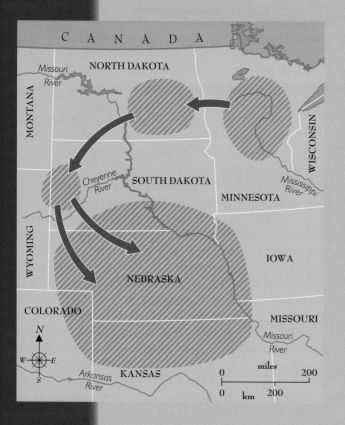

As the red areas on the map show, the Cheyennes first lived in what is now Minnesota, migrating to North Dakota in the 1600s. Pushed southwest to the Black Hills of South Dakota, they became buffalo hunters on the northern Great Plains after 1760.

who made three kinds of people in the far north — hairy people, white people, and red people. The red people followed the hairy people to the south, but the hairy people eventually disappeared. When the red people returned to the north, they found that the white people were gone. The Creator then gave the red people corn to grow and buffalo to hunt.

A Cheyenne in **powwow** dress at the Red Earth Festival. This large competitive powwow is held each June in downtown Oklahoma City.

The Language of the Cheyennes

One of the great language families of North America, the Algonquian language family includes Cheyenne, Ojibwe, Blackfoot, and Shawnee, among many others. The tribes that speak an Algonquian language are widely scattered across North America. They have been separated from each other for a long time since the days in the distant past when they all spoke the same language.

Cheyenne	Pronunciation	English
hetane	hey-than-eh	man
mahtse	maht-she	mouth
maahe	mah-hey	arrow
vaotseva	vah-oht-she-vah	deer
netse	neht-she	eagle
mahpe	mah-peh	water
nahkohe	nah-ko-hey	bear
mahtame	mah-tah-meh	food

Chapter 2

A WOODLAND PEOPLE

For hundreds of years, the Cheyennes were a woodland people living in the Great Lakes region in permanent villages. Their lifestyle, based on hunting, fishing, and farming, was similar to that of other woodland peoples.

LIFE IN THE NEW LAND

During the early 1700s, however, the Cheyennes were driven west to the northern Great Plains south of today's Canada by their enemies, the Assiniboins and Ojibwes, and became **nomadic** buffalo hunters. There they met the Sutaio tribe, a people so closely related to them they could understand each others' language. By about 1800, the Sutaios had joined the Cheyenne tribe.

The Cheyennes acquired horses from other Native American groups around 1760, becoming much more mobile. They were able to follow the buffalo herds and move camp more easily. They soon became a mighty Great Plains tribe.

During the early 1800s, however, American traders brought **whiskey** to exchange with the Cheyennes for their buffalo robes. **Alcoholism** became a big problem for the tribe.

French explorer René-Robert Cavelier, Sieur de La Salle. The Cheyennes' first contact with a European was with La Salle in 1680.

Hunting buffaloes on horseback was dangerous work requiring great skill. Horses, however, allowed hunters to cover more ground and kill more buffaloes.

THE CHEYENNE BANDS SEPARATE

The various bands of the Cheyennes became accustomed to living and hunting in different river valleys on the Great Plains. By 1832, the tribe had separated into Northern Cheyennes, who lived mainly in northern Wyoming and southeastern Montana, and Southern Cheyennes, who stayed mainly in the Arkansas and North Canadian River valleys in eastern Colorado, southwestern Kansas, and northwestern Oklahoma.

WAR ON THE SOUTHERN PLAINS

During the first half of the nineteenth century, relations between the Cheyennes and the United States were mostly peaceful.

We kill buffalo by the thousand; our women's hands are sore with dressing the robes; and what do we part with them to the white trader for? We pay them for the white man's fire-water [whiskey], which turns our brains upside down, which makes our hearts black, and renders our arms weak. It takes away our warriors' skill, and makes them shoot wrong in battle. Our enemies, who drink no whiskey, when they shoot, they always kill their foe.

Porcupine Bear, Cheyenne chief, 1831

A second Treaty of Fort Laramie was signed in 1868. Here, U.S treaty commissioners are shown with chiefs of the Cheyenne and Arapaho tribes.

In 1849, the U.S. Army established Fort Laramie in eastern Wyoming to protect American settlers traveling across the Great Plains on the Oregon Trail. Cheyennes joined many other Plains tribes in signing the Fort Laramie **Treaty** of 1851, allowing safe passage of the **immigrants** on the trail.

Everything changed, however, in 1856 when peaceful Cheyennes approaching a wagon on the Oregon Trail in Nebraska were fired on. The Cheyennes fired back, wounding the wagon driver with an arrow. In revenge, soldiers from Fort Kearney, Nebraska, attacked and destroyed a Cheyenne camp, killing eight people. The incident ignited a war with the Southern Cheyennes that would last until the 1880s.

European Diseases

In 1849, a devastating **epidemic** of cholera killed as many as one-half of the Cheyenne people, greatly reducing their power. Throughout Native American history, European diseases killed far more Indians than all other causes combined, including war. European diseases were new to Indians, and it has taken a long time for their bodies to build up a natural resistance to them.

U.S. Attacks on Peaceful Villages

Some prominent Southern Cheyenne leaders, such as chief Black Kettle, tried to pursue peace with the Americans. However, Colorado Volunteers, under the command of Colonel John Chivington, attacked Black Kettle's peaceful village in eastern Colorado in 1864, killing many women and children in an event called the Sand Creek **Massacre**.

The 1867 Treaty of Medicine Lodge, signed by the Southern Cheyennes, the Kiowas, Arapahos, and Comanches, was the federal government's first attempt to confine the Plains tribes to reservations and force them to follow the white man's lifestyle. Just a year later, Lieutenant Colonel George Armstrong Custer and the U.S. Seventh Cavalry made a surprise winter attack, destroying Black Kettle's village on the Washita River in present-day

Colonel John Chivington led the Colorado Volunteer **Militia** that carried out the Sand Creek Massacre in 1864. The U.S. Congress condemned Colonel Chivington for the massacre.

I have come to kill Indians, and believe it is right and honorable to use any means under God's heaven to kill Indians.

Colonel John Chivington, 1864

A Cheyenne record of the Sand Creek Massacre, painted on a buffalo robe. Plains Indians frequently recorded historical events with buffalo-robe paintings.

Black Kettle: A Man Betrayed

One of the few survivors of the Sand Creek Massacre, Black Kettle (about 1803–1868) was a Southern Cheyenne peace chief. His Cheyenne name was Moketavato. He had sought peace with Colonel John Chivington of the Colorado Volunteers, who told him to camp with his people at Sand Creek. When Chivington launched a surprise attack on the peace chief's village, Black Kettle tried to raise the American flag that Chivington had given him, not knowing that it was the same man who was attacking him.

Cheyenne chiefs Dull Knife (seated) and Little Wolf in 1877. The war they waged over the Bozeman Trail remains one of the only wars that the United States ever lost.

western Oklahoma. They killed many Cheyennes, including Black Kettle and his wife. By 1869, the Southern Cheyennes were forced to move to a reservation in Indian Territory in what is now Oklahoma.

WAR ON THE NORTHERN PLAINS

Meanwhile, the Northern Cheyennes, led by Little Wolf and Dull Knife, joined the Lakota Sioux, led by Red Cloud, in the war over the Bozeman Trail in the 1860s. Together, the Indians forced the U.S. Army to abandon the trail to Montana and the three army forts that had been built to protect gold miners who were **trespassing** on Cheyenne and Lakota land.

An Indian painting of the Battle of the Little Bighorn. One week after the Battle of the Rosebud, Northern Cheyennes, led by Brave Wolf and Lame White Man, helped the Lakotas destroy Lieutenant Colonel Custer's cavalry troop on June 24, 1876, at the Battle of the Little Bighorn. The entire United States was stunned.

During the 1870s, Northern Cheyennes again joined the Lakotas in war. The 1868 Treaty of Fort Laramie gave the Black Hills of South Dakota to the Cheyennes and Lakotas as their sacred lands. When gold was discovered there in 1874, however, the U.S. government sent large armies to protect the prospectors who took the land for their own. In June 1876, Northern Cheyennes and Lakotas shocked U.S. generals invading Cheyenne homelands by turning back the army at the Battle of the Rosebud and wiping out the Seventh Cavalry at the Battle of the Little Bighorn. By the late 1870s, however, the army had forced all the Plains Indians to accept reservation life.

Lean Bear

A Northern Cheyenne peace chief, Lean Bear (1813–1864), traveled to Washington, D.C., in 1863 and met President Abraham Lincoln. A year later, when he encountered troops led by Colonel John Chivington, Lean Bear attempted to show them his peace medal and papers signed by President Lincoln. Chivington's soldiers shot and killed him.

At boarding schools, Cheyenne children were forced to look, dress, and act like American children and forbidden to speak their own language or practice their religion. They had to do all the work of running the schools, all the cleaning, cooking, and farming, which provided food for the school.

Tepees provided a perfect home for the Cheyennes. They could be taken down quickly, moved many miles away, and then put back up just as quickly.

RESERVATION LIFE

By 1869, the Southern Cheyennes had been forced to share a reservation in western Indian Territory with the Southern Arapahos. There, they endured poverty, sickness, and the U.S. policy of forcing Indians to adopt white values. The U.S. government also suppressed their religious beliefs and practices and made their children attend boarding schools.

The U.S. government forced the Northern Cheyennes to move to the Southern Cheyenne reservation, promising they could return to their northern homelands if they didn't like the reservation. The largest group, 937 people, arrived in August 1877. Within two months, two-thirds of them were sick with **malaria**.

When the Northern Cheyennes wanted to return to their homeland, the government denied their request. In 1878, a large group of Cheyennes left anyway. The army killed many during their journey, but about two hundred reached their old homes. In 1884, a presidential order created the Northern Cheyenne Reservation in southeastern Montana and allowed these Cheyennes to remain.

DIVIDING AND SELLING CHEYENNE LAND

During the 1880s, the U.S. government forced the Southern Cheyennes to divide their **communal** land into small plots in a process called **allotment**. In 1892, their remaining 3.5 million acres (1.4 million hectares) were opened to white settlers. Northern Cheyennes, however, were able keep control of most of their land. Today, the tribe still owns nearly 97 percent of its reservation.

During the twentieth century, the U.S. government assumed that Native Americans would disappear as a distinct people and **assimilate** into American culture. In 1907, the Southern Cheyennes were forced to become citizens of both the United States and the new state of Oklahoma; no longer part of an independent Indian **nation**, they could not make decisions about the tribe and its future. In 1924, the U.S. Citizenship Act forced the Northern Cheyennes to also become U.S. citizens. It was only during the civil rights movements of the 1960s and 1970s that the U.S. government stopped trying to force Indians to be like white people and allowed them to govern themselves more.

Cheyennes and Arapahos on their reservation in Indian Territory. This photo was taken in 1889 near Fort Reno.

TRADITIONAL WAY OF LIFE

Chapter 3

TRADITIONAL WOODLANDS LIFE

In the Great Lakes woodlands where the tribe first lived, the Cheyennes farmed, fished, and hunted. There, they also made pottery, an art that was lost when they were forced to move to the Great Plains.

HORSES — AND LIFE — ON THE PLAINS

When the Cheyennes acquired horses in about 1760, their way of life on the Plains changed dramatically. Before the arrival of horses, Cheyenne camps, including tepees, were moved on small sleds, called travois, made of poles and dragged by dogs. Horses could pull a much larger travois, so tepees could be a lot bigger.

Horses also made buffalo hunting much easier and more productive. Hunters could travel farther and faster in search of buffaloes. With more food, children died less frequently, allowing the Cheyennes to grow into a large and powerful tribe. The Cheyennes also became an important link in the chain of

A Southern Cheyenne family in 1890. The horse is pulling a travois.

horse-trading that made horses readily available to tribes throughout the Great Plains region. Stealing horses from other tribes was also considered a great sport.

A USEFUL ANIMAL

The buffalo provided for virtually all the needs of the Cheyennes, not just for food but also for warm robes for winter clothing and blankets. The hides were used to cover tepees and were cut into strips and twisted together to make ropes. Big spoons were carved from the horns, while the **sinews** were used for bowstrings. Even the hooves were boiled to make glue.

The introduction of horses created a golden age for Plains Indians. This painting is by Frederic Remington, a white American who created many paintings of the American West.

The Cheyennes used every part of the buffalo, wasting nothing. Whites, however, slaughtered the buffaloes by the millions just to sell the hides, which were worth about one dollar each. They left the meat to rot on the Plains. By the 1880s, Americans had destroyed all the great herds of buffaloes. The Cheyennes thus lost their main source of food, leaving them near starvation and forcing them to accept reservation life.

Cheyenne women created beautiful clothing for their families. This shirt is made of tanned hide with colored beadwork. Porcupine quills decorate the handle of this spoon made from a buffalo horn.

A Cheyenne cradleboard. Cradleboards allowed a mother to work while her baby remained safe.

TRADITIONAL CHEYENNE CHILDHOOD

Family life has always been very important to the Cheyenne people. In traditional Cheyenne communities, children are surrounded by relatives of all ages and by elders who take a special interest in the children.

This did not mean, however, that the children were limited in what they could do. On the Plains, Cheyenne children were given great freedom and allowed to make decisions for themselves almost as though they were adults. This was especially true regarding horse riding. From a very early age, Cheyenne boys and girls practically grew up on horseback, becoming amazingly skilled long before they were teenagers.

Around the Cheyenne camps, young boys played with small bows and arrows, shooting at birds. Girls had dolls made by their grandmothers and played house with small tepees that were only about knee-high.

A Cheyenne mother with her child. By carrying the baby on her back, the mother can keep her hands free for other work.

COURTSHIP AND MARRIAGE

When it was time to get married, Cheyenne **courtship** could last as long as five years before the girl would agree to marry. The girl's family arranged some marriages, but many also developed out of dating and courtship. Dating always took place under the watchful eyes of her relatives.

There were no elaborate ceremonies for marriage, mainly an exchange of gifts between the families. Divorce was rare, but it was simple and quick. A woman would put her husband's belongings outside of the tepee, or a man would simply not return to her tepee, saying he had "thrown away his wife."

For this Cheyenne boy, the bow and arrow are more than toys. The rabbits and other small **game** he brings home will help feed his family.

Family Valuables or Museum Exhibits?

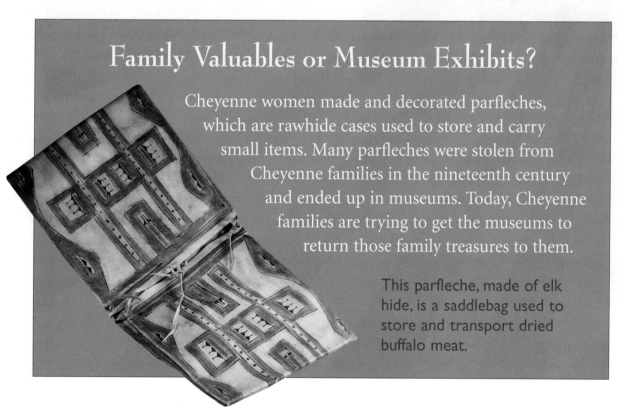

Cheyenne women made and decorated parfleches, which are rawhide cases used to store and carry small items. Many parfleches were stolen from Cheyenne families in the nineteenth century and ended up in museums. Today, Cheyenne families are trying to get the museums to return those family treasures to them.

This parfleche, made of elk hide, is a saddlebag used to store and transport dried buffalo meat.

After getting married, the man lived near his wife's relatives. His mother-in-law was forbidden to speak to him or even to look directly at him. She had to talk to him through another person, an arrangement that helped avoid conflict within the family.

TRIBAL GOVERNMENT

The Cheyennes became famous for their Council of Forty-Four, a tribal council that originally consisted of four chiefs from each of the eleven Cheyenne bands. As time went by, the number of bands decreased. Some entire bands, for example, were lost during the cholera epidemic of 1849. However, the Cheyennes maintained the tradition of having forty-four members of the council, whose main role was to settle disputes among the Cheyenne people.

A Dog Soldier. Being invited to join the Dog Soldier Society was one of the highest honors a Cheyenne warrior could achieve.

SOCIAL AND MILITARY SOCIETIES

Matters of war were left to the military societies. Nearly every Cheyenne man belonged to one of numerous different societies, which were like military and social clubs. Sometimes women were allowed to join.

The Dog Soldier Society became probably the most famous group of warriors on the Great Plains in the 1800s. Known for their bravery and skill as fighters, they were among the greatest **light cavalry** in the history of warfare. They led all other Cheyenne warriors into battle. When the tribe moved its camp, they had the high honor and great responsibility of being the rear guard.

Cheyenne women had their own societies. Being allowed to join the Quillers' Society was a high honor. Its members were responsible for maintaining high standards in making the most elaborate clothing decorated with porcupine quills and for instructing young women in the craft.

A Cheyenne painting of the Dog Soldiers. Much of the artwork of the Cheyennes was lost during the Plains wars of the nineteenth century; some of it was stolen and is now shown in museums.

Porcupine quills, some of them dyed, decorated clothing and other items.

A "Backward" Society

The most remarkable Cheyenne society is the famous Contraries. Its members were required to do most things backward, the opposite of how other people did them. Walking backward and saying good-bye when you meant hello was not a routine that everyone could learn how to do.

TRADITIONAL CHEYENNE BELIEFS

The Cheyennes believe in a Creator and in an afterlife, which is spent in the Milky Way galaxy of stars. There, Cheyennes join their dead relatives and friends.

The most important religious person in Cheyenne culture was Sweet Medicine, a Cheyenne **prophet** who traveled to Bear Butte in the Black Hills and returned with the Sacred Arrows of the Cheyennes. Bear Butte is a place where Cheyennes go to pray. Since that time, the most important Cheyenne religious event each year is the Renewal of the Sacred Arrows. It takes place in the summer on the longest day of the year. The feathers of the arrows are replaced in the ceremony. During the rest of the year, a Cheyenne elder guards the Sacred Arrows, a position of great responsibility.

SACRED MEDICINE HAT

When the Sutaio people merged with the Cheyennes long ago, they brought the Sacred Medicine Hat, another religious item of great **significance** to the Cheyennes. The Sacred Medicine Hat (sometimes called the Sacred Buffalo Hat) is entrusted to the care of a respected elder of Sutaio tribal descent. The Sutaios also shared with the Cheyennes other religious knowledge and ceremonies that are important parts of Cheyenne life, including the Sun Dance ceremony and the teachings of the Sutaio prophet named Erect Horns.

A Cheyenne buffalo medicine hat. Cheyennes learned medicine-hat rituals many generations ago from the Sutaios.

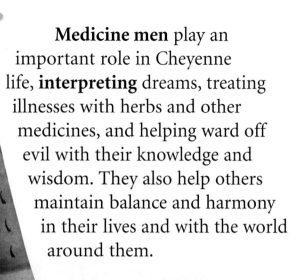

Medicine men play an important role in Cheyenne life, **interpreting** dreams, treating illnesses with herbs and other medicines, and helping ward off evil with their knowledge and wisdom. They also help others maintain balance and harmony in their lives and with the world around them.

The painting and decorations on this buckskin Cheyenne medicine tepee have religious significance.

The Sun Dance Ceremony

The Cheyenne Sun Dance ceremony each summer is an important time for the tribe. At this ritual, participants renew their promises to work for the benefit of the tribe and for the earth. The ceremonies involve going without food and water for a long time and praying and dancing for several days, all under the guidance of a medicine man who conducts the ceremonies.

Dressed for the Sun Dance, these Cheyenne men were photographed by Edward S. Curtis, a famous photographer of American Indian life, in 1911.

The Great Race

The following traditional story explains how the Cheyennes became buffalo hunters. They say that before the events in this story took place, none of the animals ate each other, and they all looked very similar.

Eventually the buffaloes and the people both decided that they wanted to be the strongest of all the animals, but to become the strongest they would have to eat other animals. So the buffaloes challenged the humans to a race to decide who would be the chief of all the animals. The humans said it would be unfair, because they only had two legs, but the buffaloes had four. They would only agree to take part if the birds could race for them.

The buffaloes agreed and they selected a young female as their runner. The humans chose four of the birds: hummingbird, meadowlark,

According to this story, the raccoon painted black circles around his eyes and tail before taking part in the race.

The black-billed magpie of this story used to be a tame species that lived close to Native American camps and ate food from people's hands.

hawk, and magpie. All the other animals decided to take part as well, just for the chance to be chief among the animals. They all painted their faces and bodies in different ways. The Cheyennes say this is why all the animals look different today.

When the race began, the hummingbird flew off very quickly, but he was soon exhausted, and the buffalo overtook him. The meadowlark took up the chase, but after a long time, buffalo pulled away into the lead. Then the hawk chased down the tired buffalo, but however hard he tried, he could not overtake her.

The last bird to speed up and chase the buffalo was the magpie. She saw the finish line in the distance and flew as steadily and strongly as she could. As they reached the line, the magpie's wings were just ahead of the buffalo's nose.

And so, the buffaloes became eaters of grass on the plains, and the people hunted them and became the most powerful of all the animals on Earth.

Chapter 4

CHEYENNE LIFE TODAY

Today, both the Northern and Southern Cheyennes retain and practice many elements of their traditional life. They also share the responsibilities of maintaining and protecting important religious items between the two tribes. The Northern Cheyennes keep the Sacred Medicine Hat, while the Southern Cheyennes guard the Sacred Arrows. The two tribes keep in close contact with each other, visiting frequently and attending each other's ceremonies and powwows.

Peyote is a spineless cactus that grows in Texas and Mexico. It has been used in Native American ceremonies for hundreds of years.

Freedom of Religion

The Native American Church, which uses a drug called peyote in its religious ceremonies, has a strong following among both the Northern and Southern Cheyennes. For many years, federal and state authorities tried to put Indians who practiced the religion of the Native American Church in jail for using peyote. Now a special law protects the religious use of peyote, which is obtained from a cactus, by members of the church.

WARRIORS AND LEADERS

Cheyennes have distinguished themselves in the twentieth century as soldiers in the U.S. armed forces in World War I, World War II, the Korean War, the Vietnam War, and the Gulf War, continuing their proud tradition as gallant fighting men. Cheyennes have also achieved distinction as leaders of political organizations and legislative bodies, including the National Congress of American Indians, where Susan Shown Harjo, a Southern Cheyenne, served as executive director from 1984 to 1987. In Congress, Ben Nighthorse Campbell, a Northern Cheyenne, was elected to the U.S. Senate from Colorado in 1992.

Senator Ben Nighthorse Campbell

When Ben Nighthorse Campbell (born 1933), a Northern Cheyenne, was elected a senator from Colorado, he became the only American Indian in the U.S. Senate. As a young man, he joined the U.S. Air Force in 1951 and served in the Korean War, learning judo while in Korea. In 1963, he won a gold medal in judo at the Pan-American Games. In 1982, he was elected to the Colorado House of Representatives and, four years later, to the U.S. House of Representatives. He became a U.S. senator in 1992.

LIFESTYLES

Many Cheyennes live and work in urban areas throughout the United States, but most continue to live on or near their reservations in Montana and Oklahoma, where their daily lives are very similar to those of other rural Americans.

Now that Cheyenne children are no longer sent away to boarding schools, they can live at home with their families and participate in powwows and other tribal activities. They now have educational opportunities that other children have while still being able to maintain their Cheyenne culture. Many Cheyennes have acquired college educations and pursue careers as managers, doctors, lawyers, and teachers.

A young Cheyenne in powwow outfit. Since judges watch many dancers compete at the same time, they track his performance by the number he is wearing.

THE NORTHERN CHEYENNES

The Northern Cheyenne Reservation was increased to its present size of 444,500 acres (180,000 ha) in southeastern Montana by a presidential order in 1900. Bordered on the west by the Crow Reservation and on the east by the Tongue River, the reservation is home to about six thousand of the approximately eight thousand tribal members.

Cheyenne tepees stand near Lame Deer, Montana, in the Northern Cheyenne Reservation, a place of great natural beauty.

While some of the land consists of steep hills and narrow valleys, much of the reservation is rich grassland and hills. Ranching and farming are the most important economic activities. The tribe also maintains herds of elk and buffalo. The Cheyenne buffalo herd was started in the 1970s and now numbers more than one hundred animals on nearly 4,000 acres (1,600 ha) of grassland. The tribe also manages 90,000 acres (36,400 ha) of forests for harvesting and selling timber.

The Northern Cheyennes have refused to allow the mining of rich coal deposits, which were discovered in 1960, on their

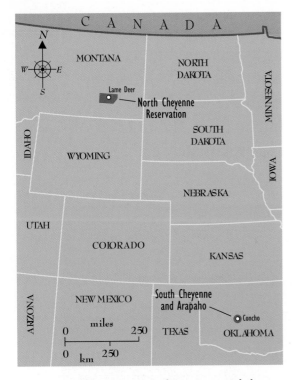

The two Cheyenne tribes are widely separated. The Northern Cheyenne Reservation lies in southeastern Montana, while the Southern Cheyennes live with the Arapahos on the Concho Reservation in western Oklahoma.

reservation. They object to the destruction of the land from open-pit mining, which occurs in areas near the reservation.

EDUCATION

After suffering several generations of being forced to attend boarding schools, the Cheyennes now maintain their own elementary school on the reservation. Older students attend the Morning Star High School. The Northern Cheyennes also operate Chief Dull Knife College, one of the tribally owned and operated institutions of higher education that make up the American Indian Consortium of Higher Education. The college is located at Lame Deer, Montana.

At Peace at Last

In 1879, U.S. Army soldiers killed thirty-one Cheyenne warriors at Hat Creek Bluffs on the northern Great Plains. Instead of allowing the Cheyennes to bury their dead relatives, the Army Medical Museum seized the bodies, kept them in boxes, and then proceeded to forget about them. It took more than one hundred years for the Cheyenne people to recover the bodies of their relatives. In October 1993, the bodies were finally returned to the Cheyennes under the Native American Graves Protection and Repatriation Act of 1990.

THE SOUTHERN CHEYENNES

Since 1869, the Southern Cheyennes have been joined with the Southern Arapahos on the Concho Reservation on the edge of the Great Plains in western Oklahoma. Known as the Cheyenne-Arapaho Tribes of Oklahoma, the two tribes govern the reservation by a joint business committee composed of representatives elected from both tribes under a **constitution** adopted in 1937.

A Southern Cheyenne in traditional dress wears a headdress made of feathers.

REDUCING THE LAND

The original reservation consisted of more than 5 million acres (2,024,000 ha). Today, only 85,000 acres (34,400 ha) remain in tribal control. Most of the land that was individually assigned to tribal members in the late nineteenth century soon passed into white hands, often by **fraud**, against which the Cheyennes were given no protection by the courts.

The Cheyennes in Oklahoma are located at the far eastern edge of the Great Plains, an area that receives much more rain than the high plains farther to the west.

During the 1950s, the Southern Cheyennes had to fight attempts by the U.S. Bureau of Indian Affairs and the U.S. Congress to end the status of their tribe as an independent nation and relocate their people to urban areas in distant cities in the United States.

A PEOPLE RECOVER

Today, the combined population of the Southern Cheyennes and Southern Arapahos is about ten thousand, of which about half live on the Concho Reservation. Many of the others live in Oklahoma City and other urban areas in the region.

Police Artist

Cheyenne artist Harvey Pratt uses his artistic skills to help solve criminal investigations. He is employed by the Oklahoma State Bureau of Investigation to create portraits of people from witnesses' descriptions and from murder victims.

When he is not using his talents to help the police he produces art and portraits on Native American subjects. He works with acrylic, oil, and watercolor paints, as well as sculpting in wood, clay, and metal.

Harvey Pratt is the great-grandson of a survivor from the Sand Creek Massacre. He is also one of the Cheyenne tribe's peace chiefs.

Harvey Pratt (right) and two other Cheyenne peace chiefs at the Red Earth Festival in Oklahoma City in 2008.

Farming and cattle raising are important economic activities. A tribally owned **casino** provides both employment for tribal members and income for tribal programs, such as health care and education.

In 2006, the Cheyenne and Arapaho Tribal college was founded on the campus of Southwestern Oklahoma State University in Weatherford, Oklahoma. It offers courses in tribal administration and in American Indian studies.

Chris Eyre

Movie director and producer Chris Eyre is a member of the Cheyenne-Arapaho Tribes. Born in 1968, he studied at New York University's film school and had his first big success in 1998 with the movie *Smoke Signals*. As in many of his movies, the action takes place on a reservation. Eyre has made movies about many aspects of Native American life, from the Arctic north to the desert Southwest. His 2003 movie *Edge of America*, about a women's basketball team on a reservation, won many awards.

Director Chris Eyre receives an award at the Directors Guild of America awards ceremony in Los Angeles in 2006.

Chapter 5

CURRENT ISSUES

Health issues are a big concern for the Cheyennes, with high suicide and diabetes rates. The tribes are also looking to improve education and transportation facilities.

SAND CREEK MASSACRE

One other issue has been ongoing for a very long time. Although the U.S. government promised the Cheyennes compensation for the Sand Creek Massacre as long ago as 1865, the tribes are still campaigning to have this money paid to them.

Members of the Southern Cheyenne and Arapaho tribes march through Washington, D.C., during a celebration of Native American culture and identity.

Southern Cheyennes in Oklahoma. Cheyenne young people have a brighter future today than at any time during the past century.

GOVERNMENT IN CHAOS

Recently, two groups in the Cheyenne and Arapaho tribal government have had very different views, and both have been trying to take overall control of tribal policy. From the end of 2010, the leadership of the joint tribes has been disputed, with each side accusing the other of **corruption**.

WIND FARMS

The Southern Cheyennes are beginning to build wind farms to make use of wind energy in Oklahoma. The first twenty-two **turbines**, built in 2011 and 2012, are designed to power the tribal headquarters, the tribal smoke shop, and a casino. The tribe plans to build many more wind farms in the near future.

Both the Northern and Southern Cheyenne people are adjusting to the great changes they have endured during the past century. They are now taking control of their lives, rather than having their lives controlled by the U.S. government. The Cheyenne people have moved confidently into the twenty-first century.

TIMELINE

before 1700	Cheyennes live in the Great Lakes region.
1680	Cheyennes' first contact with Europeans.
about 1700	Cheyennes' enemies, the Ojibwes and the Assiniboins, drive the Cheyennes toward the west onto the Great Plains.
about 1760	Cheyennes acquire horses.
about 1800	Cheyennes merge with the Sutaio people, a tribe closely related to them.
early 1800s	Cheyennes trade buffalo robes to American traders; Sioux drive the Cheyennes farther west.
1825	Cheyennes sign first treaty with the United States.
before 1832	Cheyennes divide into Northern and Southern Cheyennes.
1849	Cholera epidemic kills many Cheyennes.
1851	Cheyennes sign Treaty of Fort Laramie, allowing safe passage of settlers along the Oregon Trail.
1856	U.S. Army destroys a Southern Cheyenne village, starting a war that lasts until the 1880s.
1860s	Northern Cheyennes and Lakota Sioux at war with the United States over the Bozeman Trail.
1864	Sand Creek Massacre.
1867	Southern Cheyennes sign Treaty of Medicine Lodge.
1868	Colonel George Custer and the cavalry kill Black Kettle. Treaty of Fort Laramie.
1869	Southern Cheyennes are forced to live on a reservation in present-day Oklahoma alongside the Southern Arapaho tribe.

1872	Southern Cheyenne children are forced into boarding schools.
1876	Northern Cheyennes and Lakotas defeat U.S. forces at the Battle of the Little Bighorn in Montana.
1877	Northern Cheyennes are forced to move to Southern Cheyenne Reservation in Indian Territory.
1878	Northern Cheyennes flee from the southern reservation.
1880s	Southern Cheyennes are forced to accept land allotments.
1884	Northern Cheyenne Reservation is established in Montana.
1892	Remaining 3.5 million acres (1.4 million ha) of Southern Cheyenne Reservation sold to white settlers.
1900	Northern Cheyenne Reservation is enlarged to its present size.
1907	Southern Cheyennes are forced to become U.S. citizens.
1924	Northern Cheyennes are forced to become U.S. citizens.
1937	Southern Cheyennes adopt joint tribal constitution with Arapahos.
1950s	Southern Cheyennes fight American efforts to terminate them as a tribe and move their people to distant cities.
1960	Coal is discovered on the Northern Cheyenne Reservation; Cheyennes refuse to allow mining.
1970s	Northern Cheyennes begin building a herd of buffalo.
1992	Ben Nighthorse Campbell is elected to Senate from Colorado.
2010–2011	Serious disputes between groups in the Cheyenne-Arapaho tribal government.
2011–2012	Wind turbines are installed on Cheyenne land in Oklahoma to power structures on the Concho Reservation.

GLOSSARY

alcoholism: a disease in which people's desire to drink alcohol is so strong they cannot control it.

alien: not familiar, different.

allotment: the act of dividing land and forcing Native Americans to accept individual ownership of small farms, rather than all of the Indian land being owned by the tribe as a whole.

ancestors: people from whom an individual or group is descended.

assimilate: to force one group to adopt the culture — the language, lifestyle, and values — of another.

boarding schools: places where students must live at the school.

casino: a building that has slot machines, card games, and other gambling games.

cholera: a deadly disease that causes vomiting, diarrhea, and cramps.

communal: owned by a group of people rather than by individuals.

constitution: the basic laws and principles of a nation that outline the powers of the government and the rights of the people.

corruption: dishonest behavior by people in power.

courtship: a period when a man and a woman consider getting married.

culture: the arts, beliefs, and customs that make up a people's way of life.

discrimination: unjust treatment usually because of a person's race or sex.

environment: objects and conditions all around that affect living things and communities.

epidemic: a widespread outbreak of any serious disease.

floodplain: the area of land beside a river or stream that is covered with water during a flood.

fraud: an act of tricking or cheating.

game: wild animals hunted for food or for sport.

ice age: a period of time when the earth is very cold and lots of water in the oceans turns to ice.

immigrants: people who are moving to a new home, usually far away.

interpret: to explain the meaning of something.

irrigation: any system for watering the land to grow plants.

light cavalry: warriors or soldiers trained to fight on horseback.

malaria: a deadly disease that causes chills, high fevers, and sweating.

massacre: a brutal killing of many people.

medicine men: healers and spiritual leaders.

migration: movement from one place to another.

militia: a temporary group of fighters that is formed in an emergency to help the regular army.

nation: people who have their own customs, laws, and land separate from other nations or peoples.

nomadic: moving from place to place often.

persecution: treating someone or a certain group of people badly over a period of time.

poverty: the state of being poor.

powwow: a ceremony involving feasting, singing, and dancing.

prejudice: dislike or injustice that is not based on reason or experience.

prophet: a person who tells what will happen in the future.

reservation: land set aside by the U.S. government for specific Native American tribes to live on.

significance: importance.

sinew: a piece of tough fibrous tissue in an animal's body that joins a muscle to a bone or a bone to another bone.

tepee: a portable conical tent made of skins, cloth, or canvas on a frame of poles.

treaty: an agreement among two or more nations.

trespassing: entering someone's land without permission.

turbine: a machine whose vanes are pushed by water, wind, gas, or air, producing continuous power.

whiskey: a strong, alcoholic beverage made from barley or rye.

MORE RESOURCES

WEBSITES:

http://digital.library.okstate.edu/encyclopedia/entries/C/CH030.html
An overview of Cheyenne history and of life for the Cheyennes in Oklahoma today.

http://nativedigest.com/hpratt.html
Information about and an interview with artist Harvey Pratt, illustrated with his portraits of Native Americans.

http://www.bigorrin.org/cheyenne_kids.htm
Online Cheyenne Indian Fact Sheet For Kids in question-and-answer form with useful links.

http://www.c-a-tribes.org/historical-photograph-collection
Some historical photographs of the Cheyenne and Arapaho tribes on the official website of the Cheyenne and Arapaho tribes of Oklahoma.

http://www.cheyennenation.com/
The official website of the Northern Cheyenne tribe.

http://www.indianlegend.com/cheyenne/cheyenne_index.htm
Two Cheyenne legends.

http://www.native-languages.org/cheyenne.htm
Links to online Cheyenne language resources.

http://www.native-languages.org/cheyenne-legends.htm
Many links to Cheyenne legends and traditional stories and to books on Cheyenne mythology.

http://www.nativenetworks.si.edu/eng/rose/eyre_c.htm
A web page about the filmmaker Chris Eyre.

http://www.pbs.org/weta/thewest/program/episodes/one/dog_soldiers.htm
Briefly describes Dog Soldiers and the prophet Sweet Medicine. You can also search www.pbs.org for other information on the Cheyenne people.

Books:

Cunningham, Kevin, and Peter Benoit. *The Cheyenne (True Books)*. Children's Press, 2011.

De Capua, Sarah. *Cheyenne (First Americans)*. Benchmark Books, 2006.

Englar, Mary. *The Cheyenne: Hunter Gatherers of the Northern Plains (American Indian Nations)*. Capstone Press, 2003.

Gaines, Richard. *Cheyenne (Native Americans)*. Checkerboard Books, 2000.

Gibson, Karen Bush. *Native American History for Kids: With 21 Activities*. Chicago Review Press, 2010.

Gitlin, Marty. *The Battle of the Little Bighorn (Essential Events)*. Abdo Publishing Company, 2008.

Goble, Paul, and Rodney Frey. *Tipi: Home of the Nomadic Buffalo Hunters*. World Wisdom, 2007.

January, Brendan. *Little Bighorn (American Battlefields)*. Enchanted Lion Books, 2004.

Josephson, Judith Pinkerton. *Who Was Sitting Bull? And Other Questions About the Battle of Little Bighorn (Six Questions of American History)*. Lerner Classroom, 2011.

King, David C. *First People*. DK Children, 2008.

Murdoch, David S. *North American Indian (DK Eyewitness Books)*. DK Children, 2005.

Nashoba, Nuchi. *Ben Nighthorse Campbell: Senator and Artist (Beginning Biographies: Native Americans)*. Modern Curriculum Press, 1995.

Viola, Herman J. *It Is a Good Day to Die: Indian Eyewitnesses Tell the Story of the Battle of the Little Bighorn*. Bison Books, 2001.

THINGS TO THINK ABOUT AND DO

LIFE WITH HORSES

How many reasons can you think of to explain why nomadic people who travel a lot would find that horses make their wandering lifestyle a lot easier? List those reasons.

YOUR LIFE AT BOARDING SCHOOL

How would your school days be different if you were sent away from home and forced to live in a boarding school where nobody spoke English, where you had to help do all the cooking and cleaning at the school, and where you were not allowed to have much contact with your family? Write a few paragraphs describing what your day would be like and how you would feel.

IS A PEOPLE'S HERITAGE FOR DISPLAY?

Have you ever wondered how museums got the Indian things that are on display? Can you think of any reasons why Indian people might not be happy about some of the things that are in museums? Write an essay about your thoughts.

INDEX